YOU CHOOSE BOOKS™

Orphan Trains

An Interactive History Adventure

by Elizabeth Raum

Consultant:
Muriel Anderson, Curator
National Orphan Train Complex
Concordia, Kansas

CAPSTONE PRESS
a capstone imprint

You Choose Books are published by Capstone Press,
1710 Roe Crest Drive, North Mankato, Minnesota 56003.
www.capstonepub.com

Books published by Capstone Press are manufactured with paper
containing at least 10 percent post-consumer waste.

Library of Congress Cataloging-in-Publication Data
Raum, Elizabeth.
 Orphan trains : an interactive history adventure / by Elizabeth Raum.
    p. cm. — (You choose history)
 Includes bibliographical references and index.
 Summary: "Describes the people and events involved in the orphan trains. The reader's choices
reveal the historical details from the perspectives of a New York City newsboy, a child trying to
keep his siblings together, and a child sent west on the baby trains"—Provided by publisher.
 ISBN 978-1-4296-5479-1 (library binding) — ISBN 978-1-4296-6273-4 (paperback)
 1. Orphan trains—United States—History—Juvenile literature. 2. Orphans—New York
(State)—History—Juvenile literature. 3. Orphans—United States—History—Juvenile literature.
I. Title.
 HV985.R38 2011
 362.734—dc22   2010035015

Editorial Credits
Angie Kaelberer, editor; Bobbie Nuytten, designer; Wanda Winch, media researcher;
    Eric Manske, production specialist

Photo Credits
The Children's Aid Society, cover, 34; Corbis: Bettmann, 11; Getty Images: Museum of the City
of New York/Jacob A. Riis, 40, SSPL/Oscar Rejlander, 6, Time & Life Pictures/Nina Lears,
70; Iowa State University: Special Collections Department, 26; Kansas State Historical Society,
102–103; Library of Congress, Prints and Photographs Division, 12, 19, 37, 48, 51, 59, 79,
86, 100; National Orphan Train Complex, 17; Nebraska State Historical Society, 67; Robert
Dafford Mural at the Louisiana Orphan Train Museum, Opelousas, Louisiana, 105

The author would like to thank Sister Carol Barnes of New York Foundling for her assistance
with Chapter 4 of this book.

Printed in the United States of America in Stevens Point, Wisconsin.
052013   007391R

TABLE OF CONTENTS

ABOUT YOUR ADVENTURE

YOU are a child living in a large eastern city. Your parents are unable to care for you. You might find a new family if you travel west on an orphan train. But what if you don't find a good family? Or even worse, what if no one wants you?

In this book you'll explore how the choices people made meant the difference between life and death. The events you'll experience happened to real people.

Chapter One sets the scene. Then you choose which path to read. Follow the directions at the bottom of each page. The choices you make will change your outcome. After you finish one path, go back and read the others for new perspectives and more adventures.

YOU CHOOSE the path you take through history.

About 30,000 homeless children were living on New York City streets when the orphan train movement began.

Street Rats

The streets of New York City were filled with homeless children in the mid-1800s. The police called them street rats. Some were newly arrived immigrants. Others were born in New York. Their parents had died or were unable to care for them.

Street children supported themselves by begging or by selling whatever they could find, such as newspapers, matches, or apples. They shined shoes, gathered lumps of coal at the dockyard, or sang on street corners. Few went to school.

Turn the page.

When Methodist minister Charles Loring Brace arrived in New York in 1848, he was shocked to see these poor and abandoned children. He devoted his life to helping them. In 1853, at age 27, he became director of the Children's Aid Society.

The society did what it could to help. Brace asked young boys selling newspapers where they lived. They often replied, "Don't live nowhere!" In March 1854 Brace opened the Newsboys' Lodging House. Here newsboys could find a bed and good food for a small fee. Brace insisted that the boys attend school and religious services.

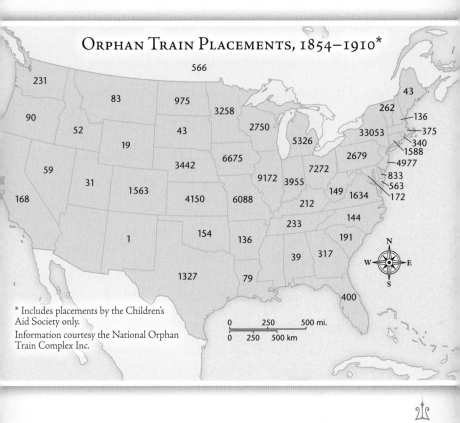

ORPHAN TRAIN PLACEMENTS, 1854–1910*

231
566
83
975
90
3258
52
2750
43
19
5326
3442
6675
59
9172
31
1563
3955
168
4150
6088
1
154
136
1327
79

43
262
136
375
33053
340
1588
2679
4977
7272
833
149
563
1634
172
212
144
233
191
39
317

400

N
W   E
S

* Includes placements by the Children's
Aid Society only.
Information courtesy the National Orphan
Train Complex Inc.

0   250   500 mi.
0   250 500 km

By 1858 Brace opened a second lodging house
for boys. In 1862 the first Girls' Lodging House
opened. The lodging houses were temporary
homes. Orphanages and prisons throughout the
city also housed homeless children.

Turn the page.

Brace believed the children would be healthier living in small towns and villages. In 1854 he began a program called placing out. A similar program in Boston sent children to work on New England farms. Brace planned to send children to communities in the western United States.

On September 28, 1854, the first group of children left New York City by train for new homes in Michigan. The group consisted of 37 boys and girls ranging in age from 6 to 15.

During the next 75 years, about 200,000 children left New York, Boston, and other cities to find new homes in the country. Another 28,000 were taken west on "baby" or "mercy" trains by the New York Foundling Hospital. The Sisters of Charity ran the hospital. The nuns chose homes for the children before they left New York City.

Children at the New York Foundling Hospital before leaving on a baby train.

Imagine that you are a child in New York.

Your parents cannot or will not take care of you.

What are your choices? How will you survive?

➻ To experience the life of a New York City newsboy in 1866, turn to page **13**.

➻ To go west in 1904 with three younger siblings, turn to page **41**.

➻ To be left alone with a baby sister in 1919, turn to page **71**.

If a newsboy didn't sell all of his newspapers, he was out the money he paid for the unsold copies.

CHAPTER 2

From Newsboy to Farm Boy

It's 4:00 a.m. on April 15, 1866. You roll out of bed, pull on your clothes, and rush to the offices of *The Sun*. The first newsboys on the street always sell their papers.

You buy 56 newspapers. If you sell them all, you'll make 28 cents profit. You'll make another 15 to 20 cents carrying suitcases for ferry passengers at the docks.

Turn the page.

Life hasn't been easy since Pa died. Ma remarried, but her new husband tossed you out on the street. "You're old enough to be on your own," he said. That was two years ago. You were 9. Until you found the Newsboys' Lodging House, you lived on the streets. Some winter nights, you slept near the heating vents that sent steam from the newspaper presses into the air. Other nights you slid down a coal chute beneath the newspaper offices and fought with other homeless children for a place near the furnace.

Now you rent a bed at the Newsboys' Lodging House on Park Place for 6 cents a night. Rent includes a bath and shampoo. Four cents buys as much pork and beans as you can eat. C. C. Tracy, the man in charge, encourages all the boys to save what they can. Maybe you'll put a few pennies in the lodging house bank.

After supper Mr. Tracy asks if anyone wants to leave the city and find a new home with a good family in the West. You're ready for a new beginning. You agree to go. Mr. Tracy is pleased.

"Mr. Charles Fry is the agent in charge," he tells you.

The night before you leave New York, the Reverend Charles Brace, who runs the Children's Aid Society, stops by to wish you well. He gives you two new sets of clothes. One is to wear and the other is to take along.

You're excited to board the train the next day. You pile onto the train with 29 other children. Some are younger than you, but most are between 10 and 12.

Turn the page.

It takes three days to reach Kalamazoo, Michigan. Mr. Fry takes you to a hotel near the station for breakfast. Then he leads you to a nearby church. You line up at the front. Dozens of people stare at you. Some are eager to adopt children. Others are just curious.

The distribution begins with a prayer and hymn sing. Then the church's minister and Mr. Fry give speeches. Eventually Mr. Fry calls for people to come forward and select a child. The smallest are chosen first. Next several older boys and girls find homes.

"Show me your muscles," a rough-looking man orders.

Reluctantly, you hold out your arm.

"Why, you're nothing but skin and bones," he growls. "Hard work will turn you into a man."

Mr. Fry steps up. "You don't have to go with this man," he says. "The decision is yours."

Orphans were given new clothes before they boarded the trains.

➤ To go with the farmer, turn to page **18**.

➤ To wait for another choice, turn to page **21**.

The farmer's name is John Jensen. You don't quite trust him, but at least you'll have a place to live.

The wagon bumps along. It takes an hour to reach the Jensen farm. Mrs. Jensen and the couple's two sons, Tom and Sam, greet you with suspicion. "He doesn't look too strong," Mrs. Jensen says as she hands you a plate of stew and hard rolls.

Tom and Sam are older than you. "We'll toughen him up," they say.

After supper Mrs. Jensen leads you to a tiny room in the attic. "Get your rest. Tomorrow you work."

Mr. Jensen wakes you at dawn and takes you to the barn. He shows you how to hitch the horse to the plow. "Plow that field over there."

In the 1800s and early 1900s, much field work was done with horse-drawn plows.

"I've never plowed before," you say.

"Then it's time you learned," he snaps.

Mr. Jensen walks along with you for a few rows, and then he leaves you on your own. The horse pulls the plow through the field, turning the soil for planting. It's hard work.

Turn the page.

You stop for lunch and then return to plowing. It takes several 12-hour days to finish the field. There's no talk of school. In fact, there's no talk at all. You miss the lively discussions at the Newsboys' Lodging House. You miss the bustle of New York's busy streets. Here on the farm, you work in silence from sunrise to sunset.

Mr. Fry visits the Jensen farm six months later. "I try to check on the boys I've placed," he says. "Tell me, how is everything going? If this is not working out, I can try to find you a new home."

Mrs. Jensen glares at you. "He's fine," she says. "There's no need to move him."

Mr. Fry turns to you. "What do you say?"

➤ To stay where you are, turn to page 22.

➤ To ask to move, turn to page 28.

You've become a good judge of character on the streets of New York. This farmer looks mean. You refuse to go with him.

Soon everyone has been chosen except you. A well-dressed middle-aged man approaches Mr. Fry.

"I'll take this boy if he wants to come with me," the man says, pointing to you. "I'm Abraham Perkins. I run the town bank."

A banker? You had hoped to live on a farm.

"You can accept Mr. Perkins' offer or continue on," Mr. Fry says. "I may be able to find you a home in the next town."

→ To continue on, turn to page 28.

→ To go with Mr. Perkins, turn to page 25.

You decide to stay with the Jensens. At least you have food and a warm bed.

One day you forget to shut the barn door. Mr. Jensen is furious. "What if the cows got out or a coyote got in? We could have been ruined!"

He punches you hard with his fists. "That will teach you," he growls. He sends you to bed without supper.

You can barely stand. You crawl up the stairs to your room. When you lie down, you have trouble breathing. Another beating might kill you. You have to run away.

To wait until morning, go to page **23.**

To sneak away that night, turn to page **32.**

You'll leave in the morning. The pain shooting through your bones keeps you awake all night.

When morning arrives, you are too sick to move. You try to stand, but you are so dizzy that you tumble back onto the bed.

"You're no good to us now," Mr. Jensen says. Tom and Sam carry you outside and dump you into the back of the farm wagon. You clench your teeth in pain at every bump the wagon makes.

Mr. Jensen pulls up at the Congregational church in town. "I can't keep this boy," he tells the minister, Harold McDonald. The minister takes one look at you, lifts you out of the wagon, and carries you into his house. "Go fetch the doctor," he tells his daughter. Within a few minutes Dr. Paul Jamison is treating your injuries.

Turn the page.

The Reverend McDonald, his wife, and daughter, Eliza, take good care of you. Soon you are able to join them at meals. You enjoy listening to Eliza play hymns on the piano.

One night the minister tells you that Mr. Fry is coming to town. "He's bringing more children with him. Perhaps you'd like to continue on with them. You'd also be welcome to stay here if you don't mind running into the Jensens from time to time."

→ *To go on with Mr. Fry, turn to page 28.*

→ *To stay with the minister and his family, turn to page 30.*

Mr. Perkins looks kind. You agree to go with him.

"My wife and I have always wanted a boy of our own. If you behave, I'll get you a dog." Mr. Perkins not only gets you the dog, but he also gives you a horse. Soon you begin calling him and his wife Pa and Ma.

Your new parents send you to school. When you turn 12, Pa lets you run errands to earn extra money. You're eager to prove that you are responsible. After all, you used to run your own newspaper business.

Turn the page.

You graduate from high school with honors. "Education is important," Pa says. "I hope you'll go on to college." Very few people have the chance to go to college. It's a wonderful opportunity. But maybe you should take a job in Pa's bank and work your way up.

Attending college was a privilege enjoyed by few people in the 1800s.

➤ To go to college, go to page 27.

➤ To begin work at the bank, turn to page 33.

Your parents are pleased when you decide to attend the University of Michigan in Ann Arbor in the fall of 1872. Pa suggests that you earn a four-year degree at the Department of Literature, Science, and the Arts. But you've been thinking of becoming a lawyer. You can enter the Department of Law and finish training as a lawyer in just two years.

➤ *To get a four-year degree, turn to page* **34**.

➤ *To study law, turn to page* **39**.

You join 12 other children going to a small farming town in western Michigan. The town hall is crowded with farmers and their wives.

"I need a hand on my farm," one man declares.

"And a girl to help in the house," says his wife.

Older boys and girls are snapped up. So are the littlest ones.

Just when you think you'll be left on stage alone, a young man steps forward. "My name is Horace Gates. My sister, Maggie, and I raise dairy cattle. I can use some help, and I'll treat you fairly."

Horace has an easy smile and seems nice. You agree to go with him. He and Maggie treat you like a little brother. Soon you are milking the cows, preparing feed for the winter, and helping Maggie make cheese and butter.

Time on the farm passes quickly from one season to the next. Five years after you arrive, Maggie marries and moves to town.

Horace talks about moving on. "I've always wanted to go to northern Michigan to work in the lumber camps. A fellow like me can earn good money. Then I'll start my own business. Do you want to come along? If not, you can mind the farm while I'm gone. You're 16 now, and I trust you."

❖ To stay at the farm, turn to page **36**.

❖ To go to the lumber camps, turn to page **37**.

You stay with the McDonalds. They treat you like a son. After looking out for yourself for so long, it's hard to feel like a kid again. But soon you get used to being part of a family. You start school as soon as you recover from the beating. Several other New York children attend school with you.

In two years you graduate from the eighth grade. The McDonalds can't afford to send you to high school, so you find work at the local stable. You enjoy working with animals. They respond well to kind words and a gentle touch. Over the years, you save your money. When the stable owner wants to sell, you are ready to buy.

One day John Jensen and his sons walk into the stables. "I'm looking to buy a horse," Jensen says with a sneer.

You stand straight and look him in the eye. "I'd never sell a horse to someone like you. You beat a poor boy half to death. Who knows what you'd do to an animal?"

Jensen is angry, but there's nothing he can do. He and his sons storm out of the stables. You're proud that you stood up to him. It almost makes up for what he did to you years ago.

THE END

To follow another path, turn to page 11.
To read the conclusion, turn to page 101.

You feel sick. It hurts to breathe. You need help now. You stumble down the steps and out the door. It's not far to the barn. You don't have the strength to lift the latch on the barn door to take the horse, so you begin walking.

The moon shines overhead as you limp along. Your eyes close, but you keep walking. It seems as if you'll make it until you trip over a rut in the road. You land with a thud, jarring your aching ribs. You try to stand, but you can't get up. You roll into the grassy field, curl up, and fall asleep.

You never wake up. You've been bleeding internally ever since Mr. Jensen broke your ribs. You die alone in a Michigan cornfield.

32

THE END

To follow another path, turn to page 11.
To read the conclusion, turn to page 101.

You begin work at the bank. First you're a teller, but soon you become assistant manager. When Pa retires, he makes you the manager. You continue to run the bank, lending money at fair rates and helping the town grow into a small city.

You marry, have a family, and become an important member of the community. You often tell your children and grandchildren how thankful you are for the opportunity provided by the Children's Aid Society.

THE END

To follow another path, turn to page 11.
To read the conclusion, turn to page 101.

Children who rode orphan trains hoped for better lives once they reached their destinations.

You're happy that you choose the four-year program. You study English, geography, history, mathematics, Latin, and Greek. The professors introduce you to exciting new ideas. You enjoy late-night discussions with other students.

When you graduate and return home in 1876, you say to Pa, "Let's open another bank. Michigan is growing. Our bank should grow along with it."

In a few years, you help Pa open four branch banks in nearby towns. The bank becomes one of Michigan's leading businesses, and Pa becomes a wealthy man. You take over when he retires.

Many years later an orphan train comes through town. You take one of the children into your own home. You hope you can do as much for him as your adoptive parents did for you.

THE END

To follow another path, turn to page 11.
To read the conclusion, turn to page 101.

You like farming, so you decide to stay. You work hard every day, but it's worth it. A few years later, you buy the farm from Horace.

When you turn 21, you marry Doris, a young woman from town. Together you expand the farm and begin a family of your own. Although you never become rich, you have everything you could want.

THE END

To follow another path, turn to page 11.
To read the conclusion, turn to page 101.

Being a logger is a great adventure. Forests cover much of northern Michigan, and furniture makers in Grand Rapids need the lumber. Life in the lumber camp is not easy, but you follow orders and become a valuable worker. You share a cabin with three other loggers. At night you play cards and tell stories. It reminds you of life at the Newsboys' Lodging House.

Loggers lived in camps close to the vast forests where they worked.

Turn the page.

After a few years, you've saved enough money to go farther west. You miss farming. The government is giving away land in Dakota Territory to people who live on it and farm it for five years. You go west and stake a claim.

In time you develop a thriving farm, marry, and have children. You're proud of what you've done, but you're even prouder of your six sons. They'll always remember you as a loving father.

THE END

To follow another path, turn to page 11.
To read the conclusion, turn to page 101.

You do well in your two years of study at the law school. After graduation you return home and open a law office. The farmers and local businessmen trust you. You also do the legal work for the bank.

In a few years, you marry and become a father. You're glad your children will have better childhoods than you did. But the Children's Aid Society gave you a chance for a better life. You'll always be grateful.

THE END

To follow another path, turn to page 11.
To read the conclusion, turn to page 101.

Orphan train riders took few possessions with them on their journeys.

CHAPTER 3

"Will Anyone Want Us All?"

It's March 6, 1904, three days after you turn 11. Pa loads you, your baby brother, and your two sisters into the wagon. He takes you to the Albany Orphan Asylum in Albany, New York.

"You children will stay here for now," he says.

"I want to go home," 7-year-old Mae cries.

"Maybe someday," Pa sighs. But you know he's not telling the truth. Pa's a tinker. He goes from town to town in his wagon mending pots and kettles. He spends weeks at a time on the road. Now that Ma is dead, he has no way to care for all of you. He signs some papers and leaves with a tear in his eye.

41

Turn the page.

"We'll be all right," you tell Mae and Bessie, who's 9. "I'll take care of you."

Three weeks after you arrive, the orphanage director calls you aside. He introduces you to Herman Clarke.

"I'm an agent of the Children's Aid Society in New York City," Mr. Clarke says. "Your father turned you over to the Children's Aid Society. He wants you to find new homes in Iowa. We'll go to New York City first where I'll pick up some other children."

You tell Mae and Bessie what's happening. "Will we all stay together?" Bessie asks.

"Probably not," you say. "But Mr. Clarke says he'll try to place us near one another."

Bessie nods, but tears spill onto her cheeks. Baby George is too young to understand.

At the train station, the big black locomotive hisses and roars. George cries when the whistle blows, but once the train leaves the station, the motion rocks him to sleep. You reach New York City later that day. You stay in a lodging house while Mr. Clarke makes arrangements for the other children who will be joining you.

Two days later you and your siblings are among 15 children who board the train. It takes two days to reach Dunlap, Iowa.

A crowd waits at the town hall. You begin singing. When the song ends, people come forward. They stand below the stage and stare up at you. Some smile. Others turn away.

A tall, well-dressed man and a woman in a flowery hat lead Bessie away. "Robert Martin is a newspaper editor. Bessie will have a good home with his family," Mr. Clarke says.

Turn the page.

Mae goes with a farm couple. "I'll visit you," you call to her.

A young woman reaches for George. "I'll take the baby," she says.

You stand all alone on the stage. You want to be brave, but seeing George leave is too much to bear. You begin to sob. "Take me too," you beg.

A farmer steps up and offers you his handkerchief. "You look like a good boy," he says. "You belong on a farm."

Mr. Clarke speaks to the woman and the farmer. When he returns, he says, "Alice Hopkins says you can stay with her until George settles in. Then I'll have to find another home for you. But if you go with Hiram Lee, you'll have a permanent home near your brother and sisters."

➺ To go with Alice Hopkins and George, go to page 45.

➺ To go with Hiram Lee, turn to page 46.

"George needs me," you say. Miss Hopkins carries the baby home. You follow.

It doesn't take Miss Hopkins long to realize that a baby is lots of work. Her sister, Ingrid Larson, and her husband, Peter, take George. They offer you a home as well, but you know they can't really afford to feed a boy your age.

When Mr. Clarke comes to check on the children, he suggests that you move to the Campbell farm where Mae lives. "Mr. Campbell can always use another worker on the farm."

✦ To join Mae at the Campbells, turn to page **50**.

✦ To move in with the Larsons, turn to page **52**.

You go with Hiram Lee. Having a permanent home near Bessie, Mae, and George seems like a wise choice.

At first the farm feels strange. It's so quiet. At night all you can hear are crickets chirping. You miss the sounds and excitement of Albany. But soon you get used to it.

Mr. Lee and his wife, Irma, treat you well. They raise pigs. Soon after you arrive, one of the sows gives birth.

"This little runt is all yours," Mr. Lee says. "See if you can fatten her up, but don't be surprised if she dies. They often do."

You soak a piece of cloth in milk and force open the little pig's mouth. You squeeze a few drops of milk into her mouth, and soon she begins to suck on the milky cloth.

Within a few weeks, the runt is too big to stay in the house. "Good work," Mr. Lee says. "Someday she'll take first prize at the county fair."

Irma Lee bakes an apple pie to celebrate. You gobble your piece and put out your plate for another slice. The Lees joke with you about growing as big as the pig. At that moment you realize that these people have become your family. You begin to call them Ma and Pa.

When Mr. Clarke visits, he tells you that George now lives with Miss Hopkins' sister and her husband, the Larsons. "He's doing well. So is Mae."

"What about Bessie?"

Mr. Clarke shakes his head. "I'm afraid her family moved. They didn't leave an address. I'll let you know if I find her."

Turn the page.

Time passes. You're a good student. Soon you graduate from eighth grade. The only high school is eight miles away in Dow City.

Students in the early 1900s who were able to go on to high school considered themselves lucky.

At dinner one night, Ma and Pa have a suggestion. "There's a teacher over in Dow City, Arnold Weber. He's looking for a boy to help with the youngest students. He's willing to take you on. You can help him in the morning and attend high school in the afternoon."

"The choice is yours. We think of you as a son. We'd be mighty proud to have you stay right here on the farm with us, but we know you'd make a fine teacher."

➤ *To go to Dow City, turn to page* **54**.

➤ *To stay on the farm, turn to page* **57**.

George is doing well. You don't need to stay to look after him. "I'll stay with Mae at the Campbells," you say.

The Campbells make you work many hours each day. Mae gathers eggs, feeds the chickens, helps with the washing and housework, and tends the garden. She even chops wood for the stove. You help with the crops and care for the cattle. It's hard work for city children.

One morning, as Mae is chopping firewood, the ax slips from her hand and slashes her foot. Her screams bring you running. Blood pours from the cut. You press your shirt to the wound and hold it tight. Then you pick up Mae and carry her to the house.

"She needs a doctor," you say.

"She'll be fine," Mrs. Campbell insists.

But she's not. Mae's foot swells. She becomes feverish. You plead with the Campbells, but they refuse to get a doctor.

Farm children were expected to help even with dangerous jobs.

➤ To stay with Mae until morning, turn to page **55**.

➤ To steal a horse and ride for the doctor now, turn to page **60**.

The Larsons encourage you to stay, so you do. You get a job after school at the hardware store and give what you earn to Mr. Larson. "Thanks, son," he says. You're happy to be with George and feel like you belong.

Sometimes at school, the other kids make fun of you. "Orphan!" they sneer. They don't invite you to their homes or let you play ball with them. It hurts, but you try to ignore them.

One day Mr. Clarke comes to visit. "I've moved Mae," he says. "The Campbells accused her of stealing."

"Mae wouldn't do that!"

"I know, but she'll be happier in a new home."

"And where's Bessie?"

Mr. Clarke shakes his head. "The Martins moved away. I heard they went to Montana, but they didn't leave an address. It's sad, but sometimes we lose track of children. I'll let you know if I hear anything."

In 1907 you graduate from eighth grade. Mr. Clarke stops by on a visit. He still doesn't know where Bessie is, but he does have good news. "The Larsons tell me you're a good student. Arnold Weber, a teacher in Dow City, is looking for a bright boy to help with the younger students in the morning. You'd also be able to go to high school in the afternoons."

The offer is a great opportunity. But instead of taking it, maybe you should start your own search for Bessie.

➻ To go to Dow City, turn to page **54**.

➻ To begin searching for Bessie, turn to page **62**.

You jump at the chance for more schooling. The Webers give you a small room of your own on the third floor of their house.

You help Mr. Weber teach the youngest students. When little Eddie Pearle finally reads an entire sentence, you cheer. You decide that you'd like to be a teacher like Mr. Weber.

Your own studies go well. Soon you're ready to graduate from high school. One day Jacob Burke, who owns the local farm supply store, stops to see you. "I could use a young man to help run the store." You had planned to go to normal school to earn a teaching degree, but working in a store would also be a good job.

➤ To go to normal school, turn to page **63**.

➤ To accept Jacob Burke's job offer, turn to page **65**.

You don't dare leave. Mae is wild with fever. Her foot is swollen and red. "Please, God, let Mae live," you pray.

By morning, Mrs. Campbell comes upstairs. "See, I told you she'd be fine," Mrs. Campbell says. "Now go do your chores."

But Mae is not fine. She's as pale as the sheet she's lying on. You can't wake her. You race to the barn and throw a halter on the horse. Before Mr. Campbell can stop you, you race to town.

When you return with Dr. John Schuler, he rushes inside, picks up Mae, and carries her to the wagon. You go with them.

Despite Dr. Schuler's efforts, Mae dies. Dr. Schuler pays for a small pine casket for Mae. The Campbells don't even come to the funeral. You're so upset that you can't even cry. First your father left you. Now Mae is gone forever.

Turn the page.

"You'll stay with us until Mr. Clarke can get here," Dr. Schuler says after writing to the Children's Aid Society.

"What a terrible loss," Mr. Clarke says when he arrives. "I think it's best if you try to move on. Hiram Lee still wants a boy to help around the pig farm. Or you could go live with Edna Walker. She has a farm near Haley and raises chickens and vegetables. She could use a helpful lad like you."

You ask him about Bessie, and he tells you that her new family moved away. "I'll try to find out where they went," he says.

To go to Hiram Lee's pig farm, go to page **57**.

To live with Edna Walker, turn to page **58**.

You've made a good choice to stay with Hiram and Irma Lee. You love living on their farm. You learn everything there is to know about raising pigs.

When you turn 18, Pa Lee tells you that you are free to leave if you want. "But we'd like to have you stay right here on the farm with us. If you'd rather build a place of your own, I'm prepared to help you do that."

→ To stay on the Lees' farm, turn to page **66**.

→ To start your own farm, turn to page **68**.

You choose to live with Edna Walker. She welcomes you to her tiny house. You sleep in the loft, a small space over the main downstairs room, on a corncob mattress. It's not very comfortable, but it's much better than living on the streets.

"You'll go to school every day," Miss Walker says, "and after school, you'll clean the chicken coops and feed the hens."

You worry about Bessie. Where is she? Maybe you should go find her. But it's hard to leave Miss Walker. She depends on you.

You graduate from eighth grade. When you turn 16, you take a full-time job with the telephone company. You like stringing telephone lines across rural Iowa.

More and more people are buying telephones. Miss Walker says she doesn't need one, but you install one anyway. Once she has a phone, she spends hours talking with her sister, Ida.

In 1912 rural Iowa had more telephones per capita than any other place in the United States.

Turn to page 69.

You sneak out of the house and hitch Old Barney to the wagon. Then you run back inside to get Mae. If Mr. Campbell catches you, he'll beat you. You've been beaten for far less. Mrs. Campbell once hit you with a cooking pot for putting your finger into the jam jar.

But this time no one catches you. You put Mae on a bed of hay and drive to town. It's after midnight when you pound on Dr. John Schuler's door. He flings open the door and helps you carry Mae inside.

"She's a very sick child," he says.

In the morning Dr. Schuler sends for the sheriff. The sheriff agrees that you and Mae shouldn't return to the Campbell farm.

In a few days, Mae is better. "She'll always walk with a limp," the doctor says, "but we caught the infection in time."

The Schulers insist you stay with them. They give you new clothes and a room of your own. Mae and the Schulers' daughter, Juliana, do everything together.

For the first time in your life, you feel wanted. Dr. Schuler treats you like a son. He even talks about sending you to college.

When Mr. Clarke, the agent, comes to visit, you ask about Bessie. "Where is she?"

"The Martins moved on. I'll see what I can find out," he says.

It's a few months later when he returns. "The Martins moved to Montana. Mr. Martin plans to start a newspaper there."

➔ *To find Bessie, turn to page 62.*

➔ *To stay with the Schulers, turn to page 64.*

"I have to find Bessie," you say.

It takes three days to reach Montana. You get off the train in Billings and begin asking if anyone knows a newspaperman named Martin. There are three Martin families in Billings, but none of them knows anything about Bessie.

You search throughout Montana. You do odd jobs washing dishes, herding cattle, and building roads. But you never find Bessie.

After three years of searching, you return to Dunlap. You find a good job with the telephone company.

➻ *Turn to page 69.*

You enroll at Iowa State Teachers College in Cedar Falls. The training course lasts two years. When you graduate, you take a job in Mason City at an orphanage. The boys remind you of yourself at that age. They look scared. They don't know what the future holds.

"I was once a boy just like you," you say. "But I didn't give up, and you shouldn't either. A good education can change your life."

You still miss your siblings, but the boys become like a family to you. You become a substitute father to every boy you teach, giving each one love and encouragement.

THE END

To follow another path, turn to page 11.
To read the conclusion, turn to page 101.

Dr. Schuler knows you are worried. He hires a private detective who traces Bessie to Montana. Now that you have an address, you write to her, and she writes back. You make plans to visit her in Montana someday.

When you graduate from high school, Dr. Schuler encourages you to go to college. He hopes you'll become a doctor, but you decide to become a social worker instead. "I want to help poor and abused children," you say. After all, you know how it feels to be beaten. You spend your life making sure that other children find homes where they feel safe and loved.

THE END

To follow another path, turn to page 11.
To read the conclusion, turn to page 101.

You accept the job in town. Mr. Burke gives you more and more responsibility. Soon you are ordering supplies, writing ads for the newspaper, and visiting important customers. "I don't know how I got along without you," he says.

You fall in love, marry, and begin a family of your own. When Mr. Burke dies, he leaves the store to you. When you retire, your sons take over the store. You'll always be sorry that your original family split up, but you're grateful for the way your life has turned out.

THE END

To follow another path, turn to page 11.
To read the conclusion, turn to page 101.

The Lees have been good to you. They are getting older and need your help even more. You stay on the farm with them

Two years later Pa Lee dies of a heart attack. You take care of Ma Lee until her death. She leaves the farm to you.

You fall in love and marry. Soon you have several children of your own. Pa taught you how to be a great dad.

Many years later you receive a letter from a woman named Priscilla Parker. She says her mother, Bessie Martin, went west on an orphan train in 1904. Bessie's new family moved to Montana. Priscilla then asks if Bessie could be your sister. She includes Bessie's address and telephone number.

Your hands shake as you dial Bessie's number. You're so happy to hear her voice again. That summer you travel to Montana. Your children and grandchildren meet Bessie's children and grandchildren. At last you are together again.

Some orphan siblings were allowed to stay in contact.

THE END

To follow another path, turn to page 11.
To read the conclusion, turn to page 101.

You love the Lees, but you want to be on your own. Mr. Lee gives you 140 acres of land, three prize pigs, and $1,000 to build your own farm. You're overwhelmed by his kindness.

You build a barn first. By the time the house is complete, you're dating a local girl named Mavis. You ask her to marry you, and she says yes. Soon you'll have to add on to the house to make room for all your children. Being a father makes you wonder how your own father could give you away. Why didn't he try harder to keep you and your siblings together? Was there more he could have done? You'll never know.

THE END

To follow another path, turn to page 11.
To read the conclusion, turn to page 101.

You save enough money to buy a small home of your own. Soon you marry and have children. You search for your father, but learn that he died a few years after he left you at the orphanage. You still hope to one day find Bessie and reunite what's left of your family.

THE END

To follow another path, turn to page 11.
To read the conclusion, turn to page 101.

The Sisters of Charity made it their mission to care for orphaned babies and children.

CHAPTER 4

The Baby Train

Mama shivers and coughs. "If anything happens to me, take Eva to the Sisters of Charity. They'll take care of you." Mama falls into a restless sleep.

Eva fusses. You feed her oatmeal, change her, and rock her to sleep. You always wanted a sister, although you wish she were closer to your age. Eva is 9 months old, and you're 12.

You sit by Mama's bed, but you soon fall asleep. When Eva cries, you spring up and light the gas lamp. You change Eva and put her back to sleep. Then you check on Mama.

71

Turn the page.

She is still, and her skin is cool. "Mama!" you cry, but she can't hear you. She died while you slept in the chair.

You run downstairs and pound on the landlady's door. She calls the police.

The workers who come and take Mama's body away wear masks. Everyone fears catching the influenza that's sweeping the country in 1919. If only Papa hadn't left on a fishing boat in July. He told Mama he'd be home in September. It's now October, and he's still not back.

You carry Eva the few blocks to the New York Foundling Hospital. It's run by the Sisters of Charity.

The nun sitting behind the hospital desk looks up as you pull open the door. "Can I help you? she asks. "My name is Sister Abigail."

"My mother said I should bring Eva to you."

You place Eva into Sister Abigail's waiting arms. You turn to go. The longer you stay, the harder it will be to leave Eva here.

"Wait," Sister Abigail says. "Won't you please stay and tell me about Eva?"

➔ *To stay, turn to page* **74**.

➔ *To leave, turn to page* **76**.

"Please follow me," Sister Abigail says. She takes Eva to a room lined with cribs and places Eva in an empty one.

"Tell me what happened," Sister Abigail says.

It's as if the nun's kindness gives you permission to cry. Once the tears begin, you are powerless to stop them. Sister Abigail hugs you. "You are not alone," she says. "Your mother was right to send you here. You can help us care for Eva and the other babies. We can use an extra pair of loving hands."

You stay with the sisters for more than a year. You miss Mama, but you know she would be proud of you for taking care of Eva and other motherless children. You go to the docks every week to check on Papa, but there's never any news.

One day Sister Abigail takes you aside. "For several years now, we have been sending children to loving Catholic families across the country. So many good people are willing to take babies into their homes and hearts. Eva is scheduled to go on the next train."

"No! You can't take Eva away."

"You want Eva to have a good life, don't you?"

Your eyes fill with tears. "Yes," you say quietly.

"Then you must let her go. You can go along if you like, but I can't promise that you'll find a home. If you don't want to leave the city, we'll find a place for you at one of our city orphanages."

→ To go on the baby train with Eva, turn to page 77.

→ To plead for more time in New York, turn to page 80.

"I must go home," you say. It took all the courage you have to bring Eva to the Foundling Hospital. The sooner you say goodbye, the better. You kiss Eva on the cheek and slip back outside.

You stop at the apartment before going to the dock to see if there is any news of your father. The landlady is waiting when you reach the apartment. "Your mother owes me rent. You have 24 hours to pay what you owe."

You step inside. Mama keeps money in a glass jar above the sink. There's only 94 cents in the jar. But there is also a crumpled piece of paper. Written on it is, "In case of emergency, contact Agnes Riley." It's in Mama's handwriting and includes an address. Who's Agnes Riley?

→ To go see Agnes Riley, turn to page 82.

→ To go to the dock, turn to page 83.

"We'll go west," you say. Sister Jessie, who supervises the baby train, is pleased. Two nuns, six nurses, and you will care for the 60 children on the train. Eva's one of the youngest. Most are between 2 and 5. The nuns have already found parents for all of the children. "We'll try to find a place for you too," Sister Jessie says.

The gentle rocking of the train puts some of the babies to sleep, but others suffer motion sickness. The passenger car begins to smell of vomit and diapers. You open a window, but soot from the train's engine pours in.

It takes a day to reach Milwaukee, Wisconsin. Dozens of couples are waiting at the station.

Turn the page.

Sister Jessie leads an eager young couple over to where you and Eva wait. "Eva will be living with the Hoffmans," she says.

Eva clings to you when Mrs. Hoffman reaches for her.

"They will provide a good home for Eva," Sister Jessie says. "You must let her go."

You have no choice. You kiss Eva and tell her to be a good girl.

Once all the little ones are placed, Sister Jessie turns to you. "I'm afraid that no family is willing to take a 13-year-old. However, one of the women who met the train teaches at a Catholic school. She's willing to give you a home, but you must agree not to visit Eva. She needs to adjust to her new family. If that is too difficult, you should return to New York. You can live at the Roman Catholic Orphan Asylum in the Bronx."

The Sisters of Charity located homes for the children at the Foundling Hospital before they went west.

➺ To return to New York, turn to page **85**.

➺ To stay in Wisconsin, turn to page **98**.

"I'm sure Papa will return soon," you say. "Give us just a few more weeks."

"One month," Sister Abigail says. "But I fear your father is lost."

You go to the docks every day to see Papa's friend Patrick Murphy. "No news is bad news," he says. "His boat must have gone down."

You know you have to do what's best for Eva. You agree to go to Texas with the group from the Foundling Hospital.

You help the nuns get the children to the train station. Most of the children are younger than 3. They have the names of their new parents sewn into the hems of their clothing. Eva's tag says "Crowley."

It's a difficult trip. Babies cry. Toddlers can't sit still. When the train reaches Bowie, Texas, dozens of families are waiting at the station.

The Crowleys give Eva a new doll. "Our baby girl died," they tell Sister Jessie. "Little Eva looks just like her."

"Will you take her older sister too?" Sister Jessie asks them.

"No, I'm sorry," Mr. Crowley says, shaking his head.

Two elderly women push forward. They came to watch the excitement. "We could take the girl," they offer.

Sister Jessie says, "If you go with them, you'll be near Eva."

"Please let us stay together," you beg. "Eva needs me."

➻ *To go with the elderly women, turn to page **91**.*
➻ *To refuse to be separated from Eva, turn to page **92**.*

Agnes Riley looks like Mama, but she is older, and she scowls. Mama never scowled.

"What do you want?" she says.

You hand her the paper. "You're my sister Mary's child?" she asks. Before you can tell her that Mama died, she snarls, "What does she want now? She's knows I don't want anything to do with her."

You turn and run. There's no help here.

The Catholic school you attend is right across the street. Sister Catherine, the principal, will know what to do.

"We'll find you a room at the orphanage," Sister Catherine says. "You can stay until your father returns."

➤ *To go to the orphanage, turn to page 84.*
➤ *To return to the apartment, turn to page 86.*

Whoever Agnes Riley is, Mama must have had a reason for not going to her for help before. You wander down to the docks looking for Patrick Murphy. He got your father the job on the fishing boat. Maybe he knows what happened. You find Patrick cleaning a bunch of freshly caught fish.

"Still no word," Patrick says.

"Mama was behind on the rent," you tell him. "I don't know what to do or where to go."

Patrick sighs. "I wish I could take you in, but there's no place in my rooming house for a young girl. Maybe you can find a job."

Turn to page 86.

You don't mind living at the orphanage. You make friends easily with the other girls, and keep busy with chores and schoolwork. There are strict rules about leaving, but from time to time you sneak away to check on Eva.

One day in 1920 you arrive at the Foundling Hospital to find Eva gone. "She has gone west on a baby train," Sister Abigail says. "She's off to have a wonderful new life."

You plead with the nun to tell you where Eva has gone, but she refuses. "She is starting over. You should do the same."

You miss Eva, but you settle into the routine at the orphanage—attending classes, doing chores, and helping the younger girls. You enjoy that, and they look up to you.

Turn to page 99.

It would be too hard to stay in Wisconsin, so close to Eva, and not visit her. If you return to New York, you can go to the docks to check for Papa.

One hundred girls live at the Roman Catholic Orphan Asylum in the Bronx. Boys have their own building. The rules are strict, but you don't mind. You have many friends, and you enjoy working with the younger children.

Turn to page 99.

You return to the apartment. You pack Papa and Mama's wedding photo and your Sunday dress in Mama's old suitcase. Then you close the door for the last time.

Young boys and girls often worked 12-hour days in factories and mills during the early 1900s.

You'll find work. Some girls sell flowers. Others sew shirts in factories. You gaze up at the signs along the street. Just then, you trip over a crack in the sidewalk. The suitcase flies out of your hand. A boy grabs it and runs.

"Stop! Thief!" you scream, but he's gone. So is the wedding picture. It's too much to bear. You sit down on the sidewalk and begin to cry.

"What's wrong, dear?" asks a woman wearing a silk dress and elegant high-button shoes.

You tell her that Mama died of influenza. She moves back a step or two and covers her mouth with her hand.

"I'm not sick," you say quickly.

"Certainly not," she says, "But you can't stay on the streets. Come with me."

Turn the page.

You follow her to the Elizabeth Home for Girls on East 12th Street. The Children's Aid Society runs it. The matron in charge welcomes you and gives you a bed in the second-floor dormitory. During the day you take a sewing class. "You'll find work as a dressmaker," the teacher says.

But your stitches are uneven and your seams pull apart. "Try typing," the teacher says, but your fingers fumble over the keys.

After a few weeks, the matron takes you aside. "A wealthy woman, Ruth Milton, needs a maid. She'll give you a room, food, and weekly wages. Or maybe you would rather go west on an orphan train to find a new home."

➜ To go west, go to page 89.

➜ To take the job as a maid, turn to page 94.

You agree to go west, but first you go to the Foundling Hospital to check on Eva. "She's growing bigger every day," Sister Abigail says. "We'll do just as your mother asked. You should go ahead."

You board a train going to Missouri. At the first stop, several children are selected. But after three stops, you are still waiting. So is a tiny girl who walks with a limp. At the last stop, a young woman agrees to take the little girl.

A middle-aged man and woman step forward. They seem nervous. "We are the Fergusons. We have no children of our own."

Just then a farm couple rushes in the door. Several children trail behind. "Are we too late?" they ask. "We need an older girl to help out."

➻ *To go with the farm family, turn to page* **90**

➻ *To go with the Fergusons, turn to page* **95**.

The farm couple's names are Frank and Sarah Applegate. You think it would be fun to be part of a large family, so you agree to go with them. Once you settle in, Mrs. Applegate piles on the chores. There's no chance to rest, and when you ask about school, she tells you that it would be a waste of time.

The agent from the Children's Aid Society promised that you would be going to school. She also told you to write directly to her if you have problems. "We can always move you to a new home if it doesn't work out," she said.

➤ *To stay, turn to page* **96**.

➤ *To write to CAS asking to leave, turn to page* **97**.

Your new home is with Martha and Edith Ramsey. At first, life with them is good. You see Eva from time to time. Her new family spoils her with clothes and toys.

As time goes on, the Ramsey sisters become ill. You do housework, cooking, laundry, and shopping. Soon you are staying home from school to care for the sisters.

Sister Jessie is shocked when she visits. "Come," she says. "You are being poorly used here." She arranges for you to live at St. Mary's Orphanage in Galveston. The nuns are good to you. You complete the eighth grade and go on to high school.

You help with the little ones at the orphanage. The sisters are grateful for your help, and the children love you.

Turn to page 99.

"But I promised Eva to the Crowleys," Sister Jessie says.

"I understand. I have a sister of my own," Mrs. Crowley says. "Will you bring us another child on the next train?"

"I'll return soon," Sister Jessie promises.

People are waiting for children at three more towns along the route. The last stop is in Peaston, Texas. Only you and Eva remain. Sister Jessie speaks to the priest.

"I know of a couple who might consider taking two children," he says.

You meet the couple, Chester and June Potts. They have a small cattle ranch. They treat you and Eva as their own daughters. You work hard, but there's also time for school and church events.

When you turn 18, you attend beauty school. You enjoy fixing and cutting hair at the local beauty shop. One of your clients introduces you to her son, David. After a few months of dating, David asks you to marry him.

After the wedding, you and David move to your own ranch. You visit your adoptive parents and Eva often. You always wonder what happened to Papa, but thanks to the Sisters of Charity, you've had a good life. So has Eva.

THE END

To follow another path, turn to page 11.
To read the conclusion, turn to page 101.

Mrs. Milton lives in a mansion. It's exciting to see how the rich live. As your responsibilities increase, so do your wages.

You return to the Foundling Hospital a few months later to check on Eva. "She's gone west on a baby train. She has a new family who loves her just as much as you do," Sister Abigail says.

"Where did she go?" you ask, but Sister Abigail won't tell you. With tears in your eyes, you return to work. There's nothing else to do.

You find a new job as a clerk at Gimbels Department Store. You rent an apartment and join friends at dances and parties. Someday you'll find Eva, but for now, you enjoy the good life in New York City.

THE END

To follow another path, turn to page 11.
To read the conclusion, turn to page 101.

You go with the childless couple, the Fergusons. They apologize for not knowing much about what children need. They buy you new clothes, shoes, and games. They even buy you a bicycle to ride to school. You're happy you chose to live with them.

As you grow older, you often think of Eva. You try to find her, but she was also adopted. No one will give you any information about her. Her new family might have even changed her name. After you marry you name your oldest daughter Eva to honor the sister you lost many years ago.

THE END

To follow another path, turn to page 11.
To read the conclusion, turn to page 101.

You are too tired to write the letter. Who would listen to you anyway? It could be worse someplace else. At least you get three meals a day. The smallest Applegate girl reminds you of Eva. Where is she now? What does she look like?

One day when you're 14, there's a knock at the door. It's your father, and he has a little girl with him. "Eva!" you cry as you scoop her in your arms. "Papa, I thought you were dead," you tell him.

"My ship crashed onto the rocky Maine coast," he replies. "It took months to refit the ship and return to New York for Eva. Then it took me more than a year to find you."

Papa takes you in his arms. "We're together now," he says. "And we'll never part again."

THE END

To follow another path, turn to page 11.
To read the conclusion, turn to page 101.

You write to Jenny Hill at the Children's Aid Society. "This placement is not working out," she tells the Applegates when she arrives.

Miss Hill places you with a German-speaking family, the Krugers. You don't speak German, and their English is quite poor, but soon you learn a few German words. Gertrude Kruger is a great cook. She teaches you to make apple strudel. The Krugers treat you like a daughter.

You stay with them until you marry at age 21. Years later you write to the Foundling Hospital to find out what happened to Eva, but no one can help you. Even though you have many children and grandchildren of your own, you always wonder about Eva, your only sister.

THE END

To follow another path, turn to page 11.
To read the conclusion, turn to page 101.

The teacher, Anne Miller, is kind and helps you with schoolwork. You graduate from high school and get a scholarship to a nursing school in Chicago. You still miss Eva, though. Before you leave, you walk to the Hoffmans' house.

A small girl answers your knock. "Can I help you? Mother is in the kitchen."

"Eva?" you say. "I'm your sister."

"I don't have a sister," the girl chirps. "But I do have a baby brother. Do you want to see him?"

"Who's there, Eva?" a woman calls.

You blow Eva a kiss and back down the steps. Eva is happy with her new family. That's all you need to know.

THE END

To follow another path, turn to page 11.
To read the conclusion, turn to page 101.

When you turn 18, you enter the convent. You find peace and joy as a Catholic nun caring for children who have nowhere else to go.

In 1935 you write to the Foundling Hospital. Several years later, you get a response. The letter says that Eva settled in Dallas, Texas, and gives you her address. Eva answers your letter. One day she and her husband visit you at the convent. You're thrilled to hug the sister you never thought you'd see again.

THE END

To follow another path, turn to page 11.
To read the conclusion, turn to page 101.

About 200,000 children had found new homes by the time the orphan train program ended in 1929.

CHAPTER 5

The End of the Orphan Trains

On May 31, 1929, three young boys rode the last orphan train to new homes in Sulfur Spring, Texas. After delivering about 200,000 children to homes in 48 U.S. states and also parts of Canada, the program ended. The United States had changed since the first orphan train reached Michigan in 1854. People found better ways to help abandoned children.

The government, as well as church and private organizations, worked to solve the problems of large cities. They improved city housing and provided better medical care. They also created laws that protected children from hard work and poor treatment.

In 1912 the U.S. government created a national Children's Bureau as part of the Department of Commerce and Labor. Today the Children's Bureau is part of the Department of Health and Human Services.

State governments began to consider laws limiting the number of out-of-state children placed in their state. Michigan passed the first such law in 1887. Other states soon followed.

Many orphans traveled west on the Atchison, Topeka, and Santa Fe railway.

In 1929 the Great Depression began when stock market prices fell about 80 percent. This stock market crash caused many companies and banks to go out of business. Many people lost their jobs. Also, drought and poor farming practices turned much U.S. farmland into a desert called the Dust Bowl. Farm families had a hard time providing for their own children. They could no longer take in homeless children.

Placing out was replaced by the foster care system. Foster homes were usually located close to the children's original homes. Children often remained in touch with their families. The new system's goal was to reunite children with their original families.

The new programs also encouraged adoption for children who couldn't be reunited with their families. This was a big change. Few children who rode the orphan trains were legally adopted, although most took their new families' last names.

Today adoption agencies don't give children to just anyone who wants them. Adoptive parents are thoroughly investigated before and after the adoption to make sure they are providing a good home.

Prospective parents met an orphan train in Opelousas, Louisiana.

The Children's Aid Society still exists in New York City. The Foundling Hospital is now called The New York Foundling. Both organizations continue to work with families that are facing difficult times. A number of other church, private, and government groups help people in need. Just like the early days of the orphan train programs, many people work together to help kids live better lives.

TIMELINE

1826—Charles Loring Brace is born in Connecticut.

1848—Brace moves to New York City to attend Union Theological Seminary.

1849—New York City's police chief reports that 3,000 children live on the streets. Some reports put the number at 10,000.

1849—Boston Children's Mission is founded.

1850—Boston Children's Mission begins placing orphan children in homes throughout Massachusetts.

1853—Brace establishes the Children's Aid Society in New York City.

1854—The first orphan train travels from New York City to Dowagiac, Michigan.

1869—The Sisters of Charity establish the New York Foundling Hospital and begin placing Catholic children with families in western and southern states.

1887—Michigan passes a law restricting adoptions; other states soon follow.

1890—Charles Loring Brace dies. His son, Charles Loring Brace Jr., takes over the Children's Aid Society.

1890—Andrew Burke, who rode an orphan train to Indiana in 1854, is elected governor of North Dakota.

1897—John Green Brady, who rode on the same orphan train as Andrew Burke, becomes territorial governor of Alaska.

May 31, 1929—The last orphan train takes three boys to Sulfur Spring, Texas.

1987—The Orphan Train Heritage Society of America is founded to preserve the history of the orphan trains.

2007—The National Orphan Train Complex opens in Concordia, Kansas.

2008—The Orphan Train Heritage Society merges with the Orphan Train Complex to create a museum and library devoted to orphan train history.

OTHER PATHS TO EXPLORE

In this book you've seen how the events surrounding orphan trains look different from several points of view.

Perspectives on history are as varied as the people who lived it. You can explore other paths on your own to learn more about what happened. Seeing history from many points of view is an important part of understanding it.

Here are some ideas for other orphan train points of view to explore:

+ Many families who took in orphans already had children of their own. How would you have felt if your parents had taken in a child from the orphan train?

+ Many of the orphans weren't really orphans at all. They still had parents and siblings in the city. What would life have been like for a brother or sister left behind?

+ The Children's Aid Society organized committees in each town that accepted children from the orphan trains. As a member of such a committee, how would you decide who should be allowed to take in orphans?

READ MORE

Flanagan, Alice K. *The Orphan Trains*. Minneapolis: Compass Point Books, 2006.

Panagopoulos, Janie Lynn. *A Faraway Home: An Orphan Train Story*. Auburn Hills, Mich.: EDCO Pub., 2006.

Reef, Catherine. *Alone in the World: Orphans and Orphanages in America*. New York: Clarion Books, 2005.

Warren, Andrea. *Orphan Train Rider: One Boy's True Story*. Boston: Houghton Mifflin, 1996.

INTERNET SITES

FactHound offers a safe, fun way to find Internet sites related to this book. All of the sites on FactHound have been researched by our staff.

Here's all you do:
Visit *www.facthound.com*
Type in this code: 9781429654791

GLOSSARY

abandon (UH-ban-don)—to leave something or someone forever

asylum (uh-SY-luhm)—an institution that cares for orphans or others needing special assistance

dormitory (DOR-muh-tor-ee)—a building with many beds or sleeping rooms

foundling (FOUND-ling)—a baby or small child without a known parent

immigrant (IM-uh-gruhnt)—a person who moves to another country to live permanently.

influenza (in-floo-EN-zuh)—an illness that is like a bad cold with fever and muscle pain; it can be deadly

matron (MAY-truhn)—a woman who is in charge at an institution

normal school (NOR-muhl SKOOL)—a teacher's training college

nun (NUHN)—a woman who lives in a religious community and has promised to devote her life to God

orphanage (OR-fuh-nij)—a place that provides a home for children without families to care for them